Diary of a War Child

The Memoir of Gertrud Schakat Tammen

as told to Diana Star Helmer

Perfection Learning®

Dedication

I dedicate this book to my only sibling, my sister Eva Waltraud Schakat Krueger, who became by best friend in adulthood. Without her, I might not have survived.

And to future generations, with a plea to do everything possible to avoid wars.

Image Credits: Images provided by Gertrud Schakat Tammen pp. 4, 47, 66, 67, 68, 69, 70. Other images copyright ArtToday (www.arttoday.com)

Cover Design: Tobi Cunningham
Inside Design: Tobi Cunningham

PB ISBN-13: 978-0-7891-5436-1 ISBN-10: 0-7891-5436-6
RLB ISBN-13: 978-0-7569-0082-3   ISBN-10: 0-7569-0082-4

5 6 7 8 9 PP 19 18 17 16 15

Table of Contents

Introduction

Gertrud Schakat Tammen was born in 1931 in northeastern Germany, which was then called East Prussia and is now part of Russia. The story of her childhood as World War II began is told in the book *Once Upon a War: The Memoir of Gertrud Schakat Tammen.*

When Gertrud was little, Germany won every battle. But when her country began losing battles, Gertrud and thousands of others lost their homes. Gertrud kept a diary of her family's search for a new home and a new life. The actual words from her diary are an important part of this book.

The war drained Germany of opportunities for young people. So in 1954, after graduating from high school and nurse's training, Mrs. Tammen came to the United States. In Iowa, she worked as a nurse, the job she'd dreamed of.

One day in 1994, Mrs. Tammen was bandaging a patient's foot. "What do you do for a living?" she asked her patient.

"I write children's books," the young woman answered.

"I kept a diary when I was a girl," said Mrs. Tammen. "I've always wanted it to be a real book."

That is how Mrs. Tammen met Diana Star Helmer, and that is how this book began.

Chapter

October 1944

Somebody bumped the suitcase in my right hand. The bag in my left hand thumped someone else. I wished I had a free hand to hang on to Mama's hand.

Mama and I had only packed what we could carry on the train. But some people had piles of bags. Some were even loading furniture on to the train!

"Oh, Mama," I breathed. "We left so much behind."

I saw regret in her eyes too. But only for a second.

"And what would we do with all our things?" Mama asked. "We don't know where we're going. We don't know who will take us in. We can't ask strangers to take us in—and our furniture too."

We boarded the train. I could smell people's faded perfume on the seats.

I almost forgot why we were leaving home. I forgot the Russian army and its bombs that were closing in on us.

In those seats, I felt as if we were on summer vacation again, riding the train to my uncle's farm. And just like in summer, I felt sure we'd be home soon.

Hitler would stop the Russians. The whole world knew our leader was almost ready to launch Germany's new wonder weapon, the *Wunderwaffe*.

> **Wunderwaffe**
> (VOON-der-vah-feh) is the German word for "wonder weapon."

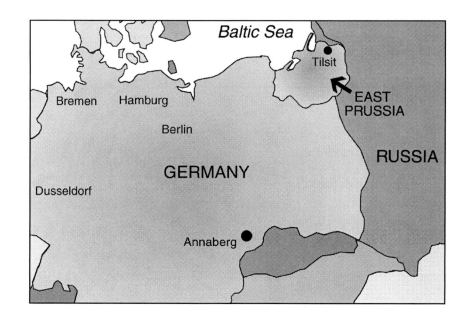

Our first **robot bomb** had hit London a couple of months ago. The English should have given up then. This new bomb would be so much better. They would all surrender—the English, the Russians. Everyone! The war would end. Mama and I could go home. And Germany would be normal again.

But while we waited, I would be going on an adventure! I'd never seen Germany's mountains. I'd never been far from home. My heart danced when the train started. *Clack, clackety-clack, clackety-clack, clackety-clack, clackety.*

I watched out the window. The trees and hills seemed to grow. The shadows in the car bent low. I leaned against Mama and tried not to think of home. It wasn't much like home now anyway. Papa and my big sister Eva were there. The government had forced them to stay.

But everyone else was gone—my best friend Heta and Inge and Gretel. They'd all gone with their families. Our town was too close to the Russian border. School had even been canceled. There weren't enough kids to make a class.

Mama and I had been among the last to leave Tilsit. We just couldn't believe the Russians would really come.

Germany had been at war with Russia since I was 10. I was 13 now. The Russians had never crossed our borders before. Maybe they never would.

I woke up. The train was slowing.

"Are we there?" I yawned.

Mama pointed out the window. I blinked at the flashing sky. Then I heard the *PUHMmmm*.

"Which city are they bombing?" I asked.

Before Mama could answer, the conductor shouted, "The train is stopping. Remain in your seats!" Then the lights went out. Now the bombers couldn't see us.

⊷⊷⊷⊷⊷⊷⊷⊷⊷

We rode through the night and another day before the conductor called the name of our stop. "Annaberg!" he shouted.

Stiff from sitting, Mama and I hobbled after everyone to a big, brick building.

"What now, Mama?" I whispered once we were inside. "How do we find out where we'll stay?"

Mama looked around. "There." She pointed the way. Clutching our bags, we lined up, gave our names, then moved aside.

We waited.

Finally, a young woman approached us.

"*Frau* Schakat?"

Mama stood. "And my daughter Gertrud."

Frau (frau) is the German word for "Mrs."

"I'm Leah Klemm," she said. "You're staying with us." And just like that, we had a new home.

Leah led us to the apartment she shared with her mother. It was one block away.

7

There was a room for Mama and me with a bed, sofa, dresser, and wood-burning stove. And there was a **gramophone**! We could play songs we wanted to hear whenever we wanted.

I felt like a guest in a hotel—even if Mama did take pots and pans out of her suitcase and cook our meals herself.

Annaberg was full of newcomers. Almost every family had taken in people like us—people running from the Russians.

I felt as if I was on an adventure! Then I went to school.

"This is Gertrud," my new teacher told the class. "She's a **refugee** from Tilsit in East Prussia."

Refugee. That sounded like someone poor. Someone who didn't have anything, or anybody. But Mama and I had each other. We had Papa and Eva and our home in our own town, Tilsit.

But no one in Annaberg knew that.

●◇ ●◇ ●◇ ●◇ ●◇ ●◇ ●◇ ●◇ ●◇

"Gertrud," Mama said after lunch one day. "All you do is sit around here. Why don't you go do something with your friends?"

I used to tell Mama everything when I was little. I didn't want to now, but . . .

"All the girls in my class have boyfriends!" I finally cried. "That's all they talk about. Nobody acted like that in Tilsit. I feel dumb here. I hate this school!"

Mama put her arms around me. Her heart beat against my ear. And I suddenly realized how quiet it was in Annaberg.

In Tilsit, I'd heard the heartbeat of **artillery** every day. Russians shot at Germans. Germans fired at Russians. In Annaberg, the silence was almost spooky.

8

Mama pulled away.

"We're going home for Christmas," she said.

"Mama!" I cried.

"Things are so quiet here," Mama said, as if reading my thoughts. "And East Prussia has been quiet since we left."

My thoughts raced. Maybe the war would really end soon. Maybe the Russians were worn out. Maybe my best friend Heta had already come home. Maybe school would start in Tilsit again. Maybe—just maybe.

"Of course, this is just to visit," Mama interrupted. "We'll come back here after Christmas."

Oh, no. Come back? But then I thought, of course. We'd come back for our things. The holiday trains would be too crowded to take our pots and pans. Or the fabric Mama had bought to make me a coat—my first new coat in years. And my two big dolls. I sewed for them, like Mama sewed for me and Eva.

I gave my dolls new names before we left. I called the girl Herta. It sounded almost like Heta. And I called the boy Peter, my old cat's name. We'd had to leave him behind in Tilsit.

Would Peter still be there? I wondered.

Chapter 2

Christmas 1944

It didn't feel like Christmas. We didn't even go home to Tilsit. Eva was working in the Braunsberg government offices. Papa's tugboat had war work in Labiau. So Mama and I went to Labiau for Christmas. After all, Papa's boat was home to us too.

But the government wouldn't let us on Papa's boat! Mama and I had to sleep in bunks on an old ship in the harbor. We shared the ship with other ship workers' families.

But we *were* together—Mama, Papa, and I. But I missed Eva. Bossy old Eva! I felt sorry for her too. She was alone at Christmas. And I felt sorry for us. We had no tree, no presents, and no relatives visiting. Nobody thought about peace on earth. How could we with a war going on?

Mama and I went to Braunsberg for New Year's. *Tante* Anna worked in Eva's office too. That meant Cousin Bruno was in Braunsberg! He was almost like a brother. New Year's seemed just like other holidays in Tilsit. Papa always had been away on his boat, and the rest of us had sat around the kitchen table, eating, talking, and laughing.

> **Tante**
> (TAHN-tuh)
> is German
> for "aunt."

Mama ruined it after a few days. "We'll have to go back to Annaberg soon," she said. "School will be starting."

"Gertrud probably misses her friends," Eva said.

I did. But I didn't miss the friends Eva meant. "I don't want to get too far behind," I said truthfully.

"You should visit Tante Lena and Tante Ida before you leave," Eva said. "They're only a few miles away. They'll be disappointed if you don't."

"What about the planes?" said Tante Anna. The table got quiet.

Russian planes had been flying over little towns like Braunsberg lately. They'd swoop down and shoot—not just at soldiers, but at other people. I'd seen it happen near Annaberg too.

Once, I was walking past a field. I'd seen a farmer stop plowing to look up. Then I heard what he heard. It was an engine. A plane dipped over the field. Gunshots rattled. Then the little plane droned away. The farmer was left, lying dead in the field.

Mama interrupted my thoughts. "We'll be careful," she said.

We made it to Tante Ida's. I didn't want to go back to Annaberg. Then suddenly, we couldn't go back. The Russians had attacked.

After all these years, the enemy was here. For the first time, the Russians had crossed our borders. Troops marched onto our land. And every day, the news said they were taking over more German cities. On January 21, they took Tilsit.

Tilsit. I thought of Russians in our neighborhood. Russians in our house. Russians who'd always been locked in the jail by my old school. Now those prisoners were free.

The Russians had taken towns to the south, east, and north. They had German roads and trains. They'd almost surrounded us.

Our government ordered women and children to get out—NOW! Papa, *Onkel* Max, and Onkel Richard had to stay to fight the Russians.

> **Onkel** (OHN-kel) is the German word for "uncle."

Mama, Tante Anna, Tante Ida, and Tante Lena gathered at Ida's table to make plans.

"The only way out is the *Frische Haff*," Mama said.

The water was frozen now that it was January. Crossing that ice was our only hope.

> ## Frische Haff
> (FRISH-eh HAHF) A long arm of land reaches out of Germany into the Baltic Sea. The water inside that arm is the Frische Haff. Ships sail from the sea into the Haff except during winter.

"There's so much snow," said Tante Ida. "Let's take the sleigh."

"No," Mama said. "Wagons still roll in snow. And sleighs are useless once the snow melts."

"There's more room in the wagon too," Eva added. "We'll need lots of hay for the horses."

So the next morning, we loaded the wagon with hay and bags for four aunts, six

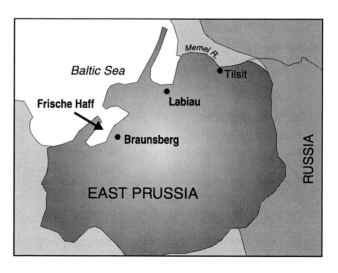

cousins, and *Oma*. Oma sat on top on a featherbed. We built a tent over the whole thing, tying the flaps against the wind.

Oma (OH-mah) is German for "Grandma."

Oma and Mama climbed inside. Tante Ida clucked to her horses. The wagon lurched forward. The rest of us pulled scarves over our frozen noses and trudged through the snow beside the wagon.

The road was cramped with wagons full of people, hand-pulled carts, and even bicycles. The wind pinched every nose and pierced every eye.

Suddenly, there were so many faces, we had to stop.

I saw soldiers in the crowd.

"Wait till you're given permission to cross!" one soldier shouted. "The ice is solid. But we must limit how many people cross at a time. Wait for further instructions."

My feet chilled. I paced. I folded and refolded my arms.

A soldier strode over to Bruno.

"How old are you?" he growled.

Tante Anna cried, "He's only 14!" She started pawing through their bags. "I have his birth certificate!"

"You'd better," the soldier smirked. "Or he'll have to stay. Germany needs soldiers."

Bruno looked so scared. He looked about 10 years old right then.

"Here it is!" Tante Anna shrieked.

The soldier squinted at the paper. Then thrust it back at Tante Anna.

"Check the wagon!" he barked.

13

Other soldiers looked for men in our wagon.

By the time they waved us on, I couldn't feel my fingers anymore. My ears hurt from listening for planes to swoop down. We were such easy targets. But I only heard horses' hooves on snow, creaking wagon wheels, and my own loud thoughts.

What if we come to thin ice? I thought. What if the wagon breaks through?

○◇ ○◇ ○◇ ○◇ ○◇ ○◇ ○◇ ○◇ ○◇

Darkness was gathering when we started gaining on the people in front of us. Crowds of people milled on the shore. The shore! We were almost there!

Almost. Holes split the ice. Vicious black water twisted inside them. Empty-eyed horses lay half in and half out of the water. Wrecked pieces of wagon bobbed around them. I tried not to look, tried not to think, tried not to do anything but walk.

At last, we were on the little strip of land that interrupted the sea. We found ourselves in a fishing village stuffed with refugees. We walked until a woman called from a doorway. "Here! You may sleep here!"

Too many bodies heated the little house. But the unknown waited outside. And I still didn't feel warm.

Chapter

Winter/Spring 1945

The next morning, the little village on the Frische Haff bustled like a city. People poured out of houses. They filled the streets. The human flood swallowed us and carried us out of town.

"M—Maybe the mainland will be warmer." Bruno's teeth chattered as we walked.

But once we reached the wider land, the people just spread out. The wind wound through my legs like a cat.

"Look!" Eva pointed. A sewing machine was leaning near the roadside. "Wouldn't Mama love that?"

In the ditch, I saw suitcases, dishes, accordions, and other things people couldn't carry anymore. So many treasures that were too heavy. We could have been rich if we had picked up those treasures. But where would they have fit in the wagon? How would we have taken them on a train?

"Don't look!" Eva hissed.

"It doesn't hurt to look," I said.

Then I saw. Piles of clothes lay on spotted snow. In the middle were faces with unseeing eyes.

I looked up, as if the plane that had killed them was still there. When I looked back, I saw German soldiers marching, shoving ragged Russian prisoners in front of them.

An old prisoner stumbled. He crouched where he fell, moaning and praying. His beard was brittle against the snow.

My heart stopped. I'm scared too, I thought. Germans. Russians. We're all scared. We all need help.

I looked back. The soldiers had left the old man to die.

We all needed help. But Germans helped Germans first. When we came to towns, they had buildings ready for refugees to sleep in. There were stables and hay for the horses. There was food, though not much. But everyone got something.

We walked for a week. My legs ached every day.

Another week passed. I lay awake at night in rooms full of strange coughs, strange snores, and strange sobs.

Another week passed. I couldn't remember what it was like to feel warm.

●◇ ●◇ ●◇ ●◇ ●◇ ●◇ ●◇ ●◇ ●◇

After about four weeks, we came to Stolp. Mama, Eva, and I took any train we could. No one used tickets. Refugees like us just jumped into empty freight cars and packed in, shoulder to shoulder.

We would jump from train to train, making our way to Annaberg. To the Klemms. To a place where someone knew us. And to where Papa could find us.

Oma and the others kept the wagon. They'd keep going west on the icy roads, looking for homes in the bombed-out towns.

Nobody said it. But we knew we might never see one another again.

●◇ ●◇ ●◇ ●◇ ●◇ ●◇ ●◇ ●◇ ●◇

It was weeks before Mama, Eva, and I saw familiar faces and buildings. But finally we arrived in Annaberg!

Leah Klemm looked confused when she opened the door and saw us.

"We didn't know when you were coming back," she said. "Or if you were coming back."

The door to our room opened. A strange woman looked out.

"This is Frau Schmidt," Leah said, not looking at us. "She's also a refugee."

The Klemms had given away our room!

"Don't worry," Frau Klemm broke in. "Let me talk to our landlady and see what we can do."

Within minutes, the landlady bustled in.

"My poor dears!" Frau Boeswetter cried. "Stay with me till we get this straightened out. Poor things! I'll get a bath for you."

A bath. We'd slept in our clothes for six weeks. We'd slept sitting up in train stations and on the ground. Undressed, my own skin looked unfamiliar.

Once in the
bath, hot
water
wrapped
around me like
arms, holding
my toes, my
ribs, my legs. The

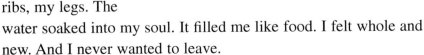

water soaked into my soul. It filled me like food. I felt whole and new. And I never wanted to leave.

When I had finished my bath, Frau Boeswetter said, "I'll sleep on the sofa. You sleep in my bed."

I stared at the clean, white sheets. I don't care what anybody says. I know what heaven will be like. Heaven will be just like that bath and that bed. I know it will.

⋄⋄ ⋄⋄ ⋄⋄ ⋄⋄ ⋄⋄ ⋄⋄ ⋄⋄ ⋄⋄ ⋄⋄

A few days later, our old room was ready for us again. And somehow, life went on. We talked. We cooked. We ate and slept.

And the Russians came closer and closer.

I don't know when we'd stopped waiting for Germany's wonder weapon. I do know we weren't surprised when the Russian army marched into town one night. When we heard the rumbling tanks, we all ran up the hill to Main Street and watched.

German women, men, and boys gathered. And no one made a sound. No one moved until the tanks had passed and the slap of Russian boots on the pavement faded. Then still silent, we walked home.

Germany **surrendered** the next day on May 9, 1945.

All the Russians in the jails were set free. The rest of the

prisoners were set free too, even murderers and robbers. The jails were emptied.

Then all these awful people—prisoners and Russian soldiers alike—ran through Annaberg looting and breaking windows. The soldiers marched through town again. Their feet pounded like ticking bombs. When would the bombs go off? When would the soldiers call every German into the street? When would they line us all up and shoot us?

Mama, Eva, the Klemms, Mrs. Boeswetter, and I didn't leave the house for days. We peeked from behind curtains at cruel-looking men shouting words we didn't understand. That's when I started my diary.

Today, on the Sunday of Pentecost, May 20, 1945, a few days after the surrender of the German Army, I am going to write about the events of the war.

Then I wrote

Peacetime

We have a **curfew** from 10 p.m. to 7 a.m. The Russian prisoners who were released are looting in the main shopping areas. We have to lock the doors. If we kill one Russian, they say that 50 Annaberg residents will be shot. The **blackout** has been discontinued. And the governor has been caught by the Russians.

Today, the Russian **infantry** and artillery personnel marched through town. Looting was going on again. Doors have to be kept locked.

When I was little, Russian prisoners had been brought to my town. They had been barefoot and wore just underwear.

We were their prisoners now.

Chapter 4

Spring 1945

Trapped indoors day after day, I wrote in my diary. But I felt as if someone was looking over my shoulder. I didn't write anything private. What if the Russians captured us and read my diary? They could punish me for writing words against them. And what if, somehow, Hitler came back to power? No, I couldn't write what I thought or felt. It wasn't safe. Nothing was safe.

May 21, 1945

This afternoon, three Russian sailors kept ringing the doorbell downstairs. We did not open it, so they finally left. The women were as scared as chickens on a ladder.

We finally had to leave the apartment. We'd run out of food.

Eva was the first to go out. Mama was too scared to go herself or to let me go. Eva always did what had to be done.

We watched out the window until she came back with a loaf of bread.

"Every time a Russian passed— even across the street—my heart raced," Eva panted. "But they don't care much about us. Let's hope it stays that way."

May 24, 1945

Miss Hoffmann, a refugee teacher from Silesia, lives in our apartment building. She got a few kids together to teach school. Public schools are closed. We are five students, three girls and two boys—all refugees.

School is great, and we are good friends most of the time.

All of the kids were from East Prussia, the same part of Germany I was from. The others were younger—9, 10, and 11. But I didn't care. It was so nice to have something to do!

Miss Hoffman gave us **dictation**. We wrote down what she said. We read aloud. I was good at school.

It was nice to feel that I was good at something.

May 26, 1945

Today, I found three lice in my hair! But, thank God, I'm not the only one. Gisela Kluge has a lot of them. Both Lehmanns have six times as many. They gave them to us. My sister also found three lice. Lehmanns contaminated the whole house with lice.

I knew the Lehmanns had traveled like us, from camp to camp. They had also been looking for shelter. It wasn't their fault. But I just wanted one corner of the world to be clean and nice.

May 29, 1945

Today, Leah Klemm has a birthday. Mama made her a blue **dirndl**. We each had a big piece of coffee cake, four cookies, and some whipped cream. They tasted heavenly!

I wrote about food a lot. That's because we didn't have any. We were all so skinny, Mama especially. It was degrading. Her clothes hung on her like she was a little girl playing dress-up.

After I wrote about the coffee cake, I realized it sounded like something else. It sounded like we had a sweet breakfast cake.

But this was a cake made from coffee grounds. Not real coffee—we couldn't get that. We made coffee out of ground-up, roasted barley. But those grounds mixed with flour, an apple, and some sugar—if you could get it—were a treat those days.

I kept writing.

There was a dance at the Bellevue Ballroom. German men were not allowed. Only German women between 18 and 35 years old.

The Russian soldiers were lonely. That's why they invited only young women to the dance. But everyone knew it wasn't safe. We'd all heard stories of Russian soldiers attacking German women.

One night, I'd heard screams in the park down the street. It was the most horrible sound I'd ever heard.

But sometimes German women did go to those dances. They thought if they were nice, maybe the Russians would give them a little more food. We were all so hungry.

Food was the first and last thing we thought about every day. I could understand a young woman getting so hungry that she'd go to the dance. But I couldn't imagine doing it myself. We were so afraid of the Russians.

I felt brave just looking at them from the window. They'd moved in up the hill from us. That's because we lived near some of the town's best houses.

One day, I saw a crowd of soldiers at the top of the hill. Then one of them started down the hill. Was he running? No, he was coming too fast. He was rolling on a bike. His legs were straight out in front of him. The handles jerked wildly.

"Mama, come quick!" I shrieked.

He crashed before she got to the window.

I was laughing so hard, all I could do was point at the

Russian dusting off his pants. His friends stampeded down the hill. Then they led their fellow soldier back to the top of the hill to do the whole thing over again.

Mama laughed till she wiped her eyes. "Russia is such a poor country," she said. "They've never had lots of nice things, like indoor water or bicycles."

We were still afraid of the Russians. But we weren't as afraid as before.

Then toward the end of May 1945, American jeeps drove down the streets of Annaberg. I followed the jeeps to the courthouse. The Russians and Americans were meeting to decide who would **occupy** Annaberg.

One of the winning countries would move soldiers into Germany to keep an eye on the new German government. We all hoped we'd get the Americans. The Russians had hated us for years.

The drivers waited in the jeeps while the officers were inside. I watched from across the street. A girl from school was watching too. We started speaking English together. We'd studied the language in school.

"Go ask him if we'll get American occupation," I dared her.

"You ask if we'll be Americans if they do," she hissed back.

"Ask him for a butter cream torte with whipped icing!" I giggled. She laughed so loud that the soldier looked at us. That made us laugh even harder.

We got Russian occupation. And the Russians wanted us out of Annaberg.

But that was all right. What we really wanted was to go home to Tilsit.

May 30, 1945

Two weeks ago, we registered with the principal of Tilsit's Queen Luise School for a transport back to Tilsit. We are supposed to leave around June 12th. Most likely in open freight cars.

June 3, 1945

Today, a transport left for Ratibor in Silesia. We hope our transport becomes reality. School has been discontinued. Hoffmanns go home to Silesia June 5.

June 5, 1945

Hoffmanns didn't get a travel permit and can't leave as of now. When we are going to be able to leave is questionable. It may take weeks, but it could happen soon.

Chapter

Summer 1945

I'd looked forward my whole life to my 14th birthday.

In Germany, little kids are called *du* until they're 14. Then they're called *sie*, like all the other grown-ups. I'd waited for my special party for as long as I could remember. All our friends and family would be there.

> **du** (DOO) is the German word for "you," used with children or close family members.
>
> **sie** (ZEE) is the German word for "you," used in formal situations and relations.

June 24, 1945

My first birthday without a cake or a party. I am 14 years old. A big disappointment. Nobody knows what is going to happen with the transport. There are hopeful and dismal hours.

We didn't even know where Papa was.

I couldn't remember the last time I'd had something new. Eva took some of our old things almost every day. She'd grab a dress, a book, or a sturdy pot. Then she'd ride a train to the country.

Eva would jump off the train when she saw a farm. Then she would walk to strange farmers' doors and try to trade for food. The farmers didn't have much either. But Eva always brought home something. She'd have some potatoes, carrots, or beets.

Sometimes, I think she stole them.

One morning before she left, Eva looked at me a long time. "Gertrud," she said gently. "Where are your dolls?"

I stood still for just a moment. Then I walked to the bed and knelt. I pulled out Herta and Peter.

I'd had them as long as I could remember.

"This dress took me four months to finish," I said.

"I know," Eva whispered.

We heard a knock. Frau Gromulies had come to go to the country with Eva.

Frau Gromulies carried Peter. Eva carried Herta.

July 8, 1945

The government posted a notice for all refugees today. We have to leave town by July 22. We won't get any **ration** cards or money after that date.

We had two weeks to get out. We thought we would go back to Tilsit. But we had no idea how we'd get there.

28

Frau Gromulies said we ought to go together. She was from Tilsit too. She had been a streetcar conductor. But we'd first met in Annaberg. We'd met lots of East Prussians here.

"We Prussians should stick together," Frau Gromulies told Mama one evening. "Now, my son Herbert knows where there's a cart. It can hold our things. We'll take turns pulling it. We can bring two boards to make a ramp for getting it on and off trains."

"Where can we buy this cart?" Mama asked.

Frau Gromulies smiled. "Herbert saw the cart at one of the Russian houses."

Mama understood then. We'd steal the cart. Why not? Russians stole from us all the time.

We shared our plans with several other families. Then we waited for a starless night. Herbert, Eva, and Frau Gromulies went to steal the cart while the rest of us packed our bags.

Later that night, we loaded our cart. And I worried.

We'd heard so many stories about Russians killing German people—torturing them. They had destroyed our churches, our schools, and our homes. They did anything that would bring us to our knees—to break us body and soul.

"Oh, Mama," I whispered. "I'm almost afraid to go back.

"The Russians took Tilsit months ago," I continued. "Will it even seem like home anymore?"

Frau Gromulies heard. She walked over and took me by the shoulders.

"Gertrud," she said as she stared into my eyes. "If those Russians have dirtied every pot in town, we'll clean them all up and start over again!"

I heard Mama laughing in the dark. And then I heard myself laugh too.

July 21, 1945

Last day in Annaberg. We left with the 11 o'clock train to Zwickau. With us were the families Gromulies, Zenteleit, Teich, Bendiks, and Kahmann. Got to Zwickau but couldn't get another connection. We had to go back to Aue and spend the night in the train. It will take us to Chemnitz in the morning. Stole a few carrots and a little lettuce from a nearby field for our supper.

I went with Eva to look for food this time. The carrots and lettuce were raw. It was hard to clean them well. Back at the train, Herbert made a face.

"I'm glad you found something for the goat to eat," he said. "But what about me?"

"What goat?" I said.

Just then, we heard rustling in the dark grass.

"That goat," Eva said. And we laughed. We knew it was just the wind. But after that, we had another traveling companion— Herbert's imaginary goat.

Riesa, July 22, 1945

Rode the train to Chemnitz and had connection to Riesa. We spent the night in the train depot's waiting room. The Poles are looting, but nothing happens to us.

Falkenberg, July 23, 1945

Had connections in the morning with the train to Wittenberg and to Berlin-Lankwitz. The train stopped often for long periods of time. The second track had been dismantled and shipped to Russia. So we had to give the right-of-way to Russian trains.

Sometimes we'd get so frustrated, going from one train to another. We'd heave the cart onto a train. Then we'd have to take it off. Then the trains would go in circles, ending up back where we'd come from. And even when signs said the place was different, everything looked the same.

Even near Berlin, the capital of Germany, there were no grand buildings, statues, or bridges. As far as I could see, there was nothing but trash. No buildings. Just bricks and boards and **rubble**. I tried so hard not to cry.

"Hey," Eva interrupted my thoughts. "Where's the goat? Don't leave it on the train by itself!"

I don't know why that made me laugh. But it did.

Berlin-Lankwitz, July 24, 1945

This morning at 5:00, we got to Berlin-Lankwitz. This is only a short hour from Berlin-Lichterfelde where Hedi Reisiger, my father's niece, lives. Their home was destroyed, so they were living with a neighbor family. After a nice visit and a good meal (they have American occupation), we spent the night in the community church hall in Lankwitz.

Berlin-Lichtenrade, July 25, 1945

From Lankwitz, they sent us to the refugee camp Lichtenrade. At noon, we got a thin cabbage soup, and in the morning and evening, we were given a slice of dry bread. After a few days, they sent us to Baruth.

We took turns looking for food. What they gave us was never enough. If we couldn't trade something, we begged in the streets for bread.

Begging was hard the first few times.

But being hungry can make you brave, if you don't let it kill you.

Day after day, we sat in the station just waiting.

We often walked out into the nearby bushes because there was no bathroom. Whenever Herbert came back, he'd say, "I just put the goat in the pasture. Maybe one of you can go check on it later."

Mama's smile sank deep in her thin, thin face. But she did smile.

Hagenow-Land, August 4, 1945

Today, we arrived at Hagenow-Land and spent the night at the train station. Haven't had a chance until now to catch up on my diary. From Lichtenrade, they took us with trucks to Baruth. From there, we were supposed to go on a train home to Tilsit.

But no such thing happened. We were allowed to stay only one night at Baruth. But there were no train connections to anywhere. The war had **rampaged** there only three months ago.

We had to walk 12 **kilometers** to Wuensdorf, where we hoped to catch a train to Berlin. We stayed there one day and begged for bread in the neighborhood. Then in the evening, we got a ride on a Russian train to Berlin. However, it stalled overnight on the tracks in Zossen.

In the morning, we got to Berlin-Tempelhof and to a tall **bunker**, which was full of bedbugs. They bit me terribly. From there, we drove through Berlin by subway and streetcar to the Lehrter railroad station.

Our hope to return to our hometown was once and forever taken from us. We cannot go home.

Everything was horrible.

Chapter 6

Fall 1945

The train stopped for a few minutes between Spandau and Nauen. Eva jumped out to tend to the goat. When she came back, she hurried to Herbert. "Here," she said. Then she dropped her watch down his boot.

Just then, two Russian soldiers jumped onto our railcar like dogs on a scent. Eva plopped onto the suitcase that had our birth certificates and important papers. My heart rolled into a ball.

One soldier marched straight over to Eva and shouted, pointing at his wrists. Eva pushed back her sleeves and shook her head. "No watch," she said.

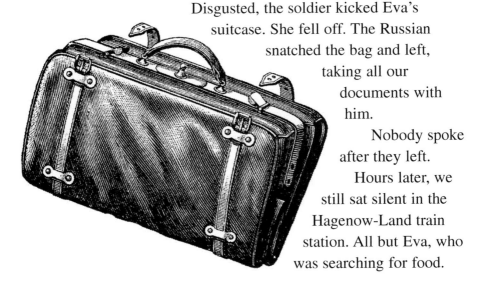

Disgusted, the soldier kicked Eva's suitcase. She fell off. The Russian snatched the bag and left, taking all our documents with him.

Nobody spoke after they left.

Hours later, we still sat silent in the Hagenow-Land train station. All but Eva, who was searching for food.

She came back with nothing.

"I don't know what to do!" Eva's voice quavered. "We've got nothing to eat. Nothing to trade. And there's nothing to trade for anyway."

Mama sat quietly. Finally she said, "God will take care of us."

"God?" Eva exploded. "Do you think God is going to walk into this station and cook us supper?"

Mama's eyes flashed. Then she looked away and shrugged.

I felt like yelling too. Eva was right. What had God done when the war started? What did God do when the bombs fell on Tilsit and we cowered in the basement and in ditches by the river? What was God doing now as we sat in bombed-out stations in garbage-pile cities?

Frau Gromulies stood. "I'd better check the goat," she mumbled.

I watched her leave. Just then two Russian women came in with bags. Before Eva even saw them, they came over to see if we had anything to trade for food.

Five minutes later, they left with Eva's silk dress. They left us with two loaves of bread!

Mama smiled. "I told you so," she said.

Hagenow-Land, August 6, 1945

We can stay here and even get ration cards. We have emergency **quarters** in the attic at Bahnhofstrasse 98.

And within just a few days, Mama, Eva, and I moved in with the Bosekes. They were a mother and a daughter. They gave us a very nice room. The Gromulieses and the others found nice families in Hagenow too.

I'm not sure what happened to the goat.

August 28, 1945

Today is my father's 59th birthday and my parents' 33rd wedding anniversary. We know nothing about his whereabouts.

September 9, 1945

Mama's birthday is today. No party, but Bosekes gave her a Bundt cake.

I started school. But it was hard to make friends. Even if I stayed, friends I made would probably leave. That's how Germany was right now.

I always went right home after school. Ingrid Boseke and I could sew for her dolls. I still loved sewing for dolls, even though I didn't have mine anymore.

October 17, 1945

We heard from Papa! He escaped from East Prussia with the *Skirwieth* (the tugboat on which he is the **machinist**). He is in Kiel and in touch with Hennings, his niece. Kiel is in West Germany, and we are trying to get over the border to be with him. This is to be accomplished with exchange transports that bring families together.

My fingers were getting **calluses** from the beautiful princess gown we were making. It had rows and rows of scalloped **embroidery**. It was all done by hand.

We finished the gown just in time.

December 6, 1945

Finally, a transport to the west is ready! All three of us get to go. We have car #3. We were supposed to leave today at 2:15 p.m., but the Russians enjoyed letting us wait.

At 9 p.m., we finally left. It was very cold in the train. It was filled over capacity.

It wasn't hard to say good-bye in Hagenow. Maybe because we'd only been there four months. Or maybe because I wanted so much to get going.

I didn't like traveling. But at least traveling was doing *something*—something that would bring us closer to making our lives like they used to be. Like they ought to be.

Herrnburg, December 7, 1945

In Schoenberg, we stopped for a short time and then went on to Luedersdorf. There we finally got some food. Three loaves of bread for five people, 50 **grams** of butter per person, two

pieces of bologna sausage, hot milk for children, and sweet coffee for adults.

Half of the trainload stayed in Luedersdorf, but we went on when it began to get dark. Next stop was Herrnburg at the border. The Russians didn't let us go over the border.

So we got out and were taken to a big warehouse with all our baggage. Even though it was dark, the Russians were not looting. We slept on straw. It was terribly cold. Snow fell that night.

Herrnburg, December 8, 1945

We stayed all day at the warehouse. And toward evening, we went to stay in a little weekend home with a family named Reimann. It was so nice and warm. We got some milk and cooked some soup. We are to go tomorrow.

Herrnburg, December 9, 1945

Today at 2 p.m., they made us gather at the road. English trucks picked us up. In the evening, we were in Luebeck-Kueknitz. We were deloused, had medical exams, and were sent off in trucks again to the refugee transit camp, Poeppendorf. They had **Quonset huts** for us. They served us a thick oatmeal soup with lots of meat in it. We slept on wood shavings.

A year earlier, the medical exam would have horrified me. Now I just put up with it. I would have done anything to get closer to Papa and to a real home.

Eutin, December 12, 1945

Today, we went to Kueknitz. Then ahead on the **autobahn**, a 1½-hour drive.

At the Reinfeld railroad depot, they gave us hard rolls, bread, milk, and coffee. Just like in paradise. From Luebeck, we were to have connections to Kiel. But we spent the night in the waiting room of the Eutin railroad station. We are supposed to go in the morning to Kiel.

Kiel, December 13, 1945

Around 9 o'clock in the morning, we arrived in Kiel. Went to Hennings. Tante Anna Henning tells us that Papa is still in Kappeln. We stay overnight.

And, the next day—

Kiel, December 14, 1945

Just by chance, the door opened and in came Papa! What a joy! After nearly a year. He is with his boat, the *Skirwieth*, in Kiel-Wik. We can't go aboard without passes. But Papa will get them for us.

Chapter

Winter 1946

We were together! Mama, Papa, Eva, and I.

Kiel, December 16, 1945

Papa brought the passes for us to go onto his ship. In the evening, I went with him. We had noodles with sugar for supper. Hmmm.

Kiel, December 17, 1945

At noon, we got orders to leave for Rendsburg at once. Papa had to get Mama and Eva from Hennings.

Rendsburg, December 18, 1945

Arrived at Rendsburg. Pretty nice town. The ship is supposed to have repairs done.

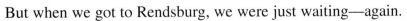

In Hagenow, I'd barely written in my journal. Once we started traveling, I wrote a lot. You never know what's going to happen when you have no home.

But when we got to Rendsburg, we were just waiting—again.

Even though we were together at last, we still were waiting for a home.

A week went by with nothing to do. Then another. I was so bored! I wasn't going to school. I had to do something. Something I could do anywhere. I couldn't sew. I needed fabric for that.

I decided to memorize something, like I used to do at Christmas. Only this would be something harder. Something grown-up. Something I would be proud to recite.

I chose "*Die Glocke*," by Friedrich von Schiller. He was one of Germany's most famous poets.

The poem was the longest one I'd ever heard. It told the different stages of building a bell and how that was like a person's life. Everyone had heard of it. But no one I knew had ever learned it by heart.

Die Glocke
(dee GLOOK-uh)
is German for
"The Bell."

I started learning the poem.

> Knowing this is in your power.
> Anyone can understand,
> What you do is what you are.
> You build your heart with your own hand.

Rendsburg, January 28, 1946

> It was decided I should go to school again. Started in Class 4 B. Teacher: Miss Oppermann. I don't like it. If it doesn't improve, I'm in trouble.

It seemed pointless to start school. I'd just have to leave. It was just what the words in "Die Glocke" said.

> All of our hopes must be mingled with fear.
> Even now, as we speak,
> Something bad may be near.

Rendsburg, January 30, 1946

When I came home from school today, we had orders **to make steam** and leave for Lauenburg-Elbe on February 1st. Nobody was happier than I was. Went to school for three days! We are supposed to stay in Lauenburg permanently.

Permanently!

I knew I shouldn't get my hopes up. But I started dreaming right away about our new home. I wondered if I'd find a best friend like Heta. What would my teachers be like?

Brunsbuettelkoog, February 1, 1946

We started sailing at 7 a.m. Now we are anchored in the harbor of Brunsbuettelkoog. The water is greenish and wavy. The pilot, who accompanied the ship, took us to town. We were able to purchase vegetables without ration cards. We bought 50 pounds of **rutabagas**, 200 pounds of green cabbage, and 50 pounds of red cabbage. Potatoes are very scarce.

Harburg, February 3, 1946

Today, we visited Trudel Keil, my father's niece. We were very happy.

Wedel, February 4, 1946

This morning, Trudel's husband brought us some flour. In the afternoon, we got orders to go back to Wedel. Lauenburg is a "NO GO."

And so we were back to where we'd started. We were waiting again.

We visited Cousin Trudel a lot. It was so nice to be in a home with Mama and family.

I started writing again when we started sailing again.

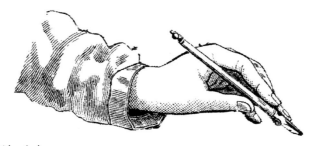

Wedel, February 28, 1946

Today, we got orders to leave for Cuxhaven on March 1st. And then on a fair day, we are to cross the North Sea to Emden.

Cuxhaven, March 1, 1946

This morning we sailed from Wedel. At Cuxhaven, the Elbe River is about seven to eight kilometers wide. The harbor is very big. We stopped at the Fishermen's Harbor.

We could go ashore only with a pass. So we got one.

The town is very nice, completely undestroyed. Bought lots of herring salad and roe and vegetable salad without ration cards. A tugboat was waiting for us. The *Skirwieth* was made seaworthy.

Seaworthy. I'd never been to sea. I had traveled only on big rivers. I wondered what the sea would be like.

Cuxhaven, March 2, 1946

Presumably, the trip across the North Sea to Emden was to start the night of Saturday, March 2nd and end on Sunday, March 3rd. But the island of Helgoland had reported high winds. So the two captains were not sure about leaving. After we came home from shopping in town, the life jackets were **getting readied**. It gave me a funny feeling.

The night trip was canceled.

North Sea, March 3, 1946

Early this morning, we were awakened by loud shouting. The captain of the Emden tugboat was asking our captain if he was ready to go. The winds were calm, so our captain agreed to take off. Papa made steam in a hurry. At 7 a.m., the tugboat took us in tow. But our engine was running also.

The sea was pretty calm. The boat only rocked a little bit. I couldn't stay under deck. It made me feel sick. Spent the whole trip on the bridge with Eva and the captain. Toward evening, the sea got a little choppy. It was pitch dark around 10 p.m. when we entered the Emden harbor.

Emden, March 4, 1946

This morning, Eva and I went to town right away. A small, muddy path led from the shipyard to town. Emden is totally demolished. Tall **air-raid** bunkers on every corner are the sole survivors of the war.

Emden, March 9, 1945

They started repair work on the *Skirwieth* today. We also got ourselves acquainted with the town.

I only wrote three more times that month, short entries about boat repairs and the ruins that used to be Emden.

I knew exactly how it had felt when the bombs hit Emden. I knew what Schiller meant when he wrote

> As in the jaws of ovens cooking
> Glows the air. The beams are cracking.
> Pillars tumbling. Windows quavering.
> Mothers wandering. Children wailing.
> All are running, saving, flying.
> Bright as day the night is shining.

Looking at the broken city, I wondered when the war would really end.

46

Chapter

Spring 1946

Papa found work in Leer! We could live on land, go to school, make friends, go to church, and just—just live! Live the way we used to live!

Emden, April 5, 1946

At noon, the journey to the new home base began. Arrived in the evening in Leer-East Friesland. The Ems River there is about as wide as the Memel in Tilsit. Leer has a population of 15,000 without refugees. We don't have an apartment yet.

Three days after we got to Leer, the *Skirwieth* got orders to sail. The only **dredging** work was in Emden, a two-hour boat ride away. That meant we'd only be in Leer on the weekends. We wouldn't be living there. During the week, we'd be on the boat. That wasn't a home at all.

Why had I let myself hope?

Gertrud's father

At night, I stood on the *Skirwieth's* deck, hearing Schiller's words in the water's lapping.

> What chain so strong, what mass so great
> Can hold the giant form of Fate?

I lived for weekends.

Easter Sunday, April 21, 1946

At 1 p.m. today, I went to see the movie *Quax, the Crash Pilot*. Saw the film the second time. Weather was very nice.

Yesterday we were given permission to spade up a piece of lawn for a garden near the warehouse. We sowed all kinds of vegetables. Now we have a place for Papa's tobacco plants.

I don't think you can plant on a sunny, spring day and not feel just a little hope. Hoeing the dirt, I said my favorite part of "Die Glocke" over and over. It's the part about falling in love.

> The eye can see the heavens open.
> The heart can feast in gentle mirth.
> Why can't it last, forever green,
> This precious moment of love's birth?

Leer, April 27, 1946

When we went to check on our garden today, the radishes were up already.

I recorded only a little in my diary. I wrote about what happened off the boat—going to the movies, gardening, and searching for food (which was still a luxury). Homey things like that were all I wanted. And they only happened on weekends.

On the Leda, May 13, 1946

Today the *Skirwieth* worked on the Leda River near Esklum at the lock. Went to some farmers, but they were **stingy** with their milk and more so with other things. Could only buy three liters. Have to go to the dentist the 18th.

On the Leda near Esklum, May 20, 1946

This is our last week at dredging operations. Work is finished, and we will be in Leer every evening. We can get two liters of milk every night from a farmer.

Leer at last! But would it last?

Leer, May 25, 1946

Our little garden is thriving. Radishes are being harvested. Today, I saw the French film *Once a Year*. It was the worst. But they showed a nice nature film about cranes.

Wore *my* new blue plaid outfit *my* mother had made for me.

A new outfit! Mama was sewing again, just like she used to.

Leer, June 1, 1946

Today, a letter from Inge Bauer! Of course, she signed it "Hummel." That's what we always called her. Hummel's letter brought sad and happy news about my friends from back home. Heta is alive and living either in Duesseldorf or Cologne. But unfortunately, no address yet. Inge Samland and her father were shot by the Russians. Hummel wants to come over to West Germany to Duesseldorf.

We still seem to have had the best fate of all.

I tried to remember we had the best fate. In bed at night, I said in my head.

Whatever the fire's rage has cost,
One comfort sweet is still unmoved.
He counts the heads of his beloved
And see! Not one dear head is lost.

I knew we were lucky. All alive, all together. The rest of our family had made it too—Tante Anna, Bruno, and the others. Yet, I felt as if someone were missing.

Sad words from "Die Glocke" were stuck in my head.

> And, oh! The children miss her care,
> Her watchful gaze and loving face.
> The orphans, left alone, must bear
> A stranger in their Mother's place.

There were strangers everywhere we went now. Germany didn't belong to Germans anymore.

Leer was run by Polish soldiers in British uniforms. They acted very important.

But I wondered, had Germany ever belonged to *Germans*?

I remembered, when I was little, clerks in stores saying they would call the police when my mother complained about war shortages. They could have too. Mama could have gone to jail, for just talking.

The old German government had terrified us, just like this new one did.

That's why I didn't write anything bad in my journal. No bad feelings or thoughts about my life. Those could be used against me if any authorities found my journal. I just kept a report. I thought that years from now, I could remember some of the feelings if I remembered the things that happened.

Leer, June 12, 1946

Today, I talked with Inga Leidig. Found out quite a bit from her about school. Tuition is 15.00 deutsche mark, very expensive. In the evening, I went to the second showing of the movie *The Great Prize*. Was very good. We sail every day to Papenburg and come back every night.

Leer, June 24, 1946

My 15th birthday passed like any other day. We had two small cakes, no company. We were underway, sailing to Papenburg. Mama gave me two blouses, one skirt, and a pair of house slippers. From Mr. Koehn and Plauschin, I got 10.00 deutsche mark. Went to confirmation class and had Miss Funke today.

Leer, June 27, 1946

When one gets used to a place, one has to leave. Had to excuse myself today from confirmation class for four weeks. The *Skirwieth* is being sent to Emden. After that, we are to return to Leer. Had Miss Funke again today. When we come back, she wants to go with us for a day. She thinks life on a ship would be great.

I didn't tell her what *I* thought. Life on a ship was the worst.

Chapter

Summer 1946

My first journal entry back in Emden pretty much summed up my feelings.

Emden, June 28, 1946
Today toward evening, we arrived in Emden in pouring rain. Everything is bleak.

Emden, June 29, 1946
Went to town today. Passes were ready for us. Used Mama's ration card. Papa lost his. Mama went scrounging for food in Borsum. Brought about seven pounds of green beans home.

I wondered if there'd ever be a time when we wouldn't worry about food every minute of every day. If there'd be a time when we wouldn't need ration cards or passes to travel in our own country. Sometimes, it seemed as if we were still at war.

Emden, July 1, 1946

During the night, an atom bomb was tested on an island of the Marshall Island group.

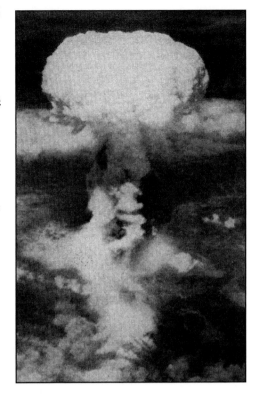

Maybe a war never really ends. But war or not, life goes on each day. Looking for food and working for food never stops, no matter what.

Today is the first working day in Emden. We dredge at the outer harbor. We have to haul away the barges filled with mud. Many foreign ships unload their freight here. Mostly British, Danes, and Norwegians. They unload potatoes and grain and reload with coal.

Emden, July 2, 1946

The weather has improved now. It's pretty hot.

We urge the captain to go alongside ships, but he doesn't dare to. After much push and shove, he went alongside one ship which was loaded with barley. We swept up about eight pounds of grain that was spilled on deck.

This grain gets ground up in the coffee grinder and turns into beautiful flour.

After work was done, we tied a ladder outside the ship. Mr. Koehn, the ship's boiler man, went swimming. Eva went down, too, though neither of us can swim. Even with a life vest, she was afraid to let go of the ladder. I had to wait till she was done because I have to use her swimsuit. First I was afraid to let go of the ladder. But soon I did. The swim vest carried me. The water was warm. Finally, I was tied to a rope without a life jacket and let down into the water. I just took one turn. As a reward, I got an egg from the dredge foreman.

Emden, July 4, 1946

Today, we went alongside an English potato ship, the *Eminence*. The harbor police are very watchful. We only succeeded in getting one pail of fresh potatoes on board. In the afternoon, we went alongside a ship loaded with wheat and got about five pounds. This way, we have a little to add to our food. We can't buy pasta or legumes in Emden.

Tonight, we went into the water again. Swimming with a life jacket is good.

Emden, July 6, 1946

Every Friday night, we go into the shipyard and stay over the weekend. Otherwise, nothing new.

Emden, July 9, 1946

Eva registered herself and me to pick peas. Went today. We earn 3.00 deutsche mark per 100 pounds picked. Minimum daily output has to be 100 pounds. Special rations for workers were 100 grams of bread, 50 grams of meat, and 15 grams of butter. You can take home five percent of the peas you pick. But we took home more than that. At night, they take us home by trucks. The tugboat anchors at night at the outer harbor.

While picking peas, my hands were busier than my mind. I started reciting "Die Glocke." I couldn't get through the whole thing. I had to think long and hard to get some of the words to come.

I thought I knew this poem! But when life is going on, it's easy to forget even things you know well.

I promised myself I wouldn't forget again.

Emden, July 19, 1946

Today, we went to pick peas again. I have been going for five days now, and I've made 18.80 deutsche mark. Mama went along today and helped, so we picked a whole lot. At night, we go into the state shipyard. It's going to be a long time until we get to go back to Leer.

Emden, July 30, 1946

It's very stormy with high waves. Woke up this morning from the rocking of the ship and the sound of waves. I thought we'd upset. One porthole was not closed, and the water splashed in. Quite a bit of water in the salon. No more waves are splashing in now, but the ship rolls terribly.

Emden, August 4, 1946

Today, the weather is nice. In the afternoon, we raised a racket with two boys who work on the boat. Got soaked twice, first on deck and then in the rowboat. Was good to have fun.

We were especially happy because this was to be the end of our work in Emden. In just one month, we were going to Leer for good—not just for weekends. We'd find an apartment and register for school. I could hardly wait for September!

Emden, September 2, 1946

This morning, we got orders to stay another two weeks, hauling rocks. We almost had a stroke! When the two weeks are gone, we'll probably get another two weeks. It's disgusting. We are looking forward to Leer so much.

I thought of the words about the bell at the end of "Die Glocke." I said them in my head all day.

Listen. Can you hear her tone
Start loud, then swiftly fade away?
"Forever" is a word unknown.
For nothing earthly ever stays.

Nothing earthly. Like a home. Nothing earthly stays.

Chapter

Fall 1946

Why didn't I figure it out sooner? Our home was earthly, just like "Die Glocke" said. And we lost it. Nothing earthly ever stays.

But maybe homelessness was earthly too! And, just like the hunger and hopelessness in the train station, the homeless times would pass too.

Emden, September 7, 1946

This morning, I was awakened by Papa saying, "We are dismissed from Emden and go back to Leer on Tuesday." That was some joy! Mama and I took the 9:30 streetcar to the outer harbor for a last stop. We went **gleaning** for grain, peas, and beans. At 3 p.m., Eva came to get us with Papa's bicycle, and we were home at 4:30.

Of course, *that* home was only the ship. In just a few days, we'd really be home at last. And life could begin again.

Leer, September 11, 1946

At 4 p.m., we arrived in Leer in pouring rain. I went right away to the movies. *Traumerei von Schumann* was good.

Almost right away, life was good too.

Leer, September 12, 1946

At Papa's office, they told me that the parish had called about my confirmation class. It's nice to be with Miss Funke. When they have some work for the *Skirwieth*, we go. Otherwise, we just lie in the harbor.

But only the boat lay in the harbor. We could play around town. This was the town that could finally become ours.

I was becoming friends with some girls. I had confirmation class. I liked Miss Funke. Eva was looking for work. Mama and Papa were looking for apartments.

Leer, September 22, 1946

Eva and Edith Waidlauski accepted jobs today to sew mattresses. They were supposed to start today. But as of now there is no work.

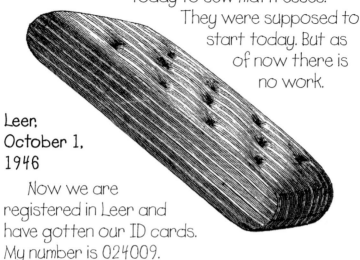

Leer, October 1, 1946

Now we are registered in Leer and have gotten our ID cards. My number is 024009.

Today is the sentencing in the Nuremberg trial. The Nazis who led the war are being tried for their crimes. Out of the 21 accused, 11 are to die by hanging.

Schacht, von Papen, and Fritsche were declared not guilty and set free. Everyone is upset about that. And people are calling for harder punishment. Among those sentenced to death were Goering, Streicher, Raeder, Saukel, Jodl, Seys, Inquart, and Borman.

I thought about when I was little. That was five years ago in Tilsit. My teacher would tell the class to listen to the radio news. We'd hear about these men who were on trial now.

We'd hear how these men were helping our leader, Hitler, save Germany. They were to save us from hunger, unemployment, and homelessness.

I'd believed the radio. My own mother said that before I was born, she'd seen many German people who were homeless and hungry. Hitler came to power when I was two. So I grew up surrounded by people with jobs, homes, and food. Everyone—my teachers, my mother, and the radio—said that Hitler made things better.

All I ever heard on the radio back then was news about Hitler's good works. Even when Germany went to war, Hitler said it was self-defense.

But now the radio told other things. Things Hitler hid for all those years. How he ordered his men to kill people—not just enemy soldiers, but other people too. Millions. Then he had lied about their deaths.

And every day, the things we heard were more horrible than the day before. I would walk alone after listening and think about Schiller's words.

> Man fears the lion's kingly tread.
> Man fears the tiger's fangs of terror.
> But of all awful things we dread,
> Man is the worst, when he's in error!
> No torch, no fire can give sight to
> the blind! Why place it in his hand?
> It helps him not, but it consumes
> the city and the land!

Hitler's war had consumed our cities and our land. But we were still here. We, the Germans. Some of us had survived.

Leer, October 14, 1946

Today, we started dredging at the Leerport bridge. The temporary bridge is being removed.

63

There'll be a ferry from Emden.
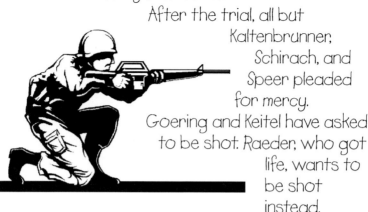
After the trial, all but Kaltenbrunner, Schirach, and Speer pleaded for mercy. Goering and Keitel have asked to be shot. Raeder, who got life, wants to be shot instead.

Leer, October 17, 1946

Today is Eva's birthday. Mama baked some cakes. Eva can't miss work, so she will celebrate her birthday Sunday the 20th at Edith Weidlauski's.

The sentenced people were executed last night between 1 and 3 a.m. Goering committed suicide with cyanide at 3:23 p.m. The bodies will be buried at sea in a secret place.

Leer, October 21, 1946

Instead of being buried at sea, the bodies have been cremated, and the ashes will be blown with the wind.

They said Goering had the poison capsule on his body since his arrest. At the time of death, only Streicher declared himself a National Socialist and ended his life saying, "Heil Hitler." Only Franke said a prayer.

We already have two beds, but no stove yet.

I looked at what I had written that day and almost laughed. First I'm writing about the horrifying deaths of hateful criminals. Then, suddenly, I tell about our new beds and new stove.

But it made perfect sense. Those men didn't defeat us. They lied to us. They let our homes be destroyed. They frightened us and broke promises and left us to fight an enemy they had made.

But we still had hope. We *had* cleaned up every pot and started over.

Leer, October 29, 1946

Today, Papa got a purchase permit for a little stove. Went and bought it right away. It was 70.00 deutsche mark with stovepipe.

We moved the stove into our little apartment and lit it. Smelling food cook on it for the first time, I thought of the end of "Die Glocke." That's where the bell is finished at last. It's rung for the very first time.

Pull ye, pull ye, heave!
The bell doth move, doth wave.
Joy to this place, she is bringing.
Peace is the first chime she's ringing.

Schiller ended his poem with peace. For us, peace was a beginning.

Afterword

We were home at last—on land. I wasn't drifting anymore! And soon, our lives were ours again. They were like I remembered in Tilsit.

Papa kept working on his ship. Mama got hold of a sewing machine and was soon making clothes again. Eva found a job as a secretary. I started school. Life was wonderful!

I put my diary away. I had friends to talk to now. I had school. And did I love school! I loved problems with right and wrong answers.

Graduating class of 1950. Gertrud—front row, fourth from left

And I started to love a boy named Frank. But I didn't know then it was love. I only knew we were friends.

I graduated in the spring of 1950. I signed up right away at our local nursing school. And I remembered *Fraulein* Motzkus, our neighbor in Tilsit. I'd always said I wanted to be a nurse just like her.

Nursing school made me admire Fraulein Motzkus even more. My

Fraulein (FRAU-lyn) is German for "Miss."

days began at 6:30 a.m. and ended at 8:00 p.m. I had no time to spend with Frank. We broke up in the fall of 1950.

I worked in every department of the hospital. Surgery was my favorite. I got As in every course.

Then in November 1952, I had an unexpected visitor.

Frank's mother came to invite me to Frank's birthday party! I accepted, wondering if Frank had accepted my love of nursing.

We became engaged one year later on Frank's 23rd birthday. It was a wonderful end to a wonderful year.

I graduated in 1953. In the summer, Frank and I visited my sister, Eva, in southern Germany. Eva and I became friends during that

Graduating from nursing school in 1953. Gertrud—front row, fourth from left

visit—real friends. I was no longer that little brat sister. We were on an equal level now, both grown up.

But growing up wasn't easy. Everyone knew jobs were scarce in Germany. Frank wanted to go abroad. He wanted to go to Canada, Australia, or best of all, the United States. He had distant relatives and a friend in Iowa.

Two weeks after our engagement, Frank left on a boat for New York City. One year later, I took the same voyage.

New York was what Berlin must have been before the war, bombs, and rebuilding. Except New York was even bigger, grander, and more frightening. I didn't understand a word of English, and I'd studied it for

From left: Gertrud, Frank, and Johanna

years! People spoke so fast and used new words. Still, I knew I would love America.

67

I watched the cities, mountains, forests, and fields flow by the train window on the way to Iowa. Frank had found good work there. Marshalltown, Iowa, greeted us with Christmas music and pretty decorations. It made me homesick for Tilsit. But I knew this was home now.

We got married in a little country church in the small town where Frank's cousins lived. We all had lunch after the ceremony. I started work in a hospital a few days later. My new husband worked as a bricklayer with a big construction company.

Four months later, war disrupted our lives again. Frank was drafted into the United States army. I was already expecting our first child.

We only saw each other twice for a few days during the next two long years. But when Frank came home in the spring of 1957, the good life was ours at last.

We bought a house. It was my first real home since Tilsit. This was the home I felt no one could take. My home.

We had three beautiful daughters, Dorie, Ingrid, and Linda. I went back to work when our youngest started school. I was an assistant in a foot doctor's office for almost 30 years until my retirement in 1999.

Front row, from left: Hannelore, Lieselotte, Inge S. Back row, from left: Inge B., Gertrud, Heta, and Gretel

In 1996, I received an amazing letter. It was from my best friend, Heta! Soon after, I heard from Inge and Gretel.

Gretel had asked a newspaper to publish a picture of us and our friends who had lived in the apartments in Tilsit. She hoped to find readers who knew where those girls might be.

My cousin Bruno sent Gretel my address. After 52 years, we found each other!

Frank and I had visited Germany a few times over the years. But all of our old friends were scattered. And we could never go back to Tilsit. It was part of Russia now.

On one trip "home," my sister Eva handed me a notebook.

"I found this in Mama's belongings after she died," Eva said.

It was my old journal.

Back home in Iowa, my children wanted me to translate my diary from German to English for them. Then they said I should write a book.

I was almost 70 when my book was published. But I could still say parts of "The Bell" by heart. And I still remembered Mama's words in the train station that someone is looking out for us. Just when you think you're lost, two enemies will appear with bread. Or an imaginary goat will make you laugh.

Gertrud and Frank

Glossary

airraid   attack by armed airplanes

artillery   cannons

autobahn   expressway or highway through Germany; similar to an interstate

blackout   period of darkness enforced as a precaution against air raids

bunker   protective embankment often made of dirt or concrete

callus   hard, thickened spot on the skin

curfew   period during which certain people are not allowed in specific areas

dictation   act of saying words that are to be written down

dirndl   dress with short sleeves and a gathered skirt

dredge   to dig to make deeper or larger

embroidery   decorative stitches sewn by hand or sewing machine

gramophone   early phonograph

gettingreadied   being prepared (German and Dutch expression)

glean   to gather leftover grain or produce

gram   metric measurement of weight in which one gram is equal to 0.035 ounce

infantry   soldiers trained, armed, and equipped to fight on foot

kilometer   metric measurement of distance in which one kilometer is equal to 0.62 mile

machinist	worker who operates or repairs machines
occupy	to take control of
quarters	place to stay; lodging
Quonsethut	premade shelter set on a foundation of bolted steel beams and built of a semicircular roof of corrugated metal
rampage	continue in a wild or violent manner
ration	food allowed for one day
refugee	person who flees to another country or location to avoid danger or persecution
robotbomb	first guided missile ever used; often called the *V-1 rocket*
rubble	broken up pieces of buildings caused by destruction
rutabaga	turniplike vegetable with a large yellowish root
stingy	not generous; unwilling to share
surrender	to give up completely
tomakesteam	to build a fire in a furnace in order to boil water, which then turns into steam. Steam pushes and turns the engine on a steamship, making the ship move.
Wunderwaffe	After launching the V-1 and the V-2 rocket, Hitler promised Germany this even better weapon. He never kept this promise.